Road Rage To Road Sage

10 Spiritual Lessons You Can Learn in LA Gridlock

James WilderHancock

WHP

Copyright © 2024 James WilderHancock

All rights reserved. No portion of this book may be reproduced in any form without written permission from the publisher or author, except as permitted by U.S. copyright law.

ISBN: 979-8-218-57672-1 (Paperback)

This book is intended for informational and educational purposes only. The author and publisher are not responsible for any actions taken based on the content of this book. The stories and examples included reflect personal experiences and perspectives; individual results or interpretations may vary.

Front cover image by James WilderHancock.
Book design by WHP.
Printed by KDP in the United States of America.
First printing edition 2024.

WHP 147 N Ave. 18 Los Angeles, CA 90031

For Colby, Mars and Kyin.
May this be some small assistance in navigating the roads ahead of you.

Contents

Copyright

Preface

Introduction

Patience in Gridlock	1
Finding Joy in the Journey	9
The Power of Breath	16
Listening to Inner Guidance	23
Letting Go of Anger	31
Letting Go of Judgment	38
Learning From Mistakes	45
Instant Karma	53
Be Like Water	60
Trail Angels	67
Practicing Gratitude	75
Conclusion	83
Acknowledgements	87
THANK YOU!	89
Tune-Up Topics	91

Preface

I never expected to write this book. I never expected to write ANY book! Yet, here I am, sharing with you what hours spent bumper-to-bumper have taught me—not just about patience and frustration, but about life itself. This book was born out of countless commutes through the sprawling roadways of Los Angeles, each one a microcosm of human behavior and emotion.

At first, like most people, I approached this infamous web of traffic with dread. It was nothing more than an obstacle, a necessary evil on the way to my destination. But over time, I began to notice something deeper: the way a moment of kindness from a stranger could change the entire day, how a breath taken in frustration could transform the moment, or how a sudden intuitive nudge could prevent disaster or provoke delight. Each traffic jam, lane change, and unexpected detour offered a lesson —sometimes humorous, sometimes poignant, and too often enraging—about resilience, connection, and personal accountability.

I realized these experiences weren't just about getting from point A to point B. They were about navigating life's broader journey. Whether it was letting go of judgment, practicing gratitude, or simply learning to breathe through the chaos, each commute became a spiritual classroom or self-help therapy session.

This book is for anyone who has ever felt trapped in a situation—on the road or off—and wondered if there might be a better way to handle it. I invite you to travel with me through these stories, drawn from my own experiences and those of friends and fellow travelers. Together, we'll explore how the lessons learned on the road can transform not just our driving, but our lives.

May you find your own path from road rage to road sage. Just maybe you've found your guide.

—JWH, Pasadena, CA 12/24/2024

"It is not the road ahead that wears you out; it is the grain of sand in your shoe."

— Arabian Proverb

Introduction

Embracing The Journey, One Mile At A Time

If you live in Los Angeles, or any major city for that matter, you know what it means to face traffic. There's something about watching brake lights stretch into infinity, moving at a crawl—or not moving at all—that can bring out a cocktail of frustration, impatience, and even helplessness. But what if the hours we spend on the road could serve a purpose beyond simply getting from point A to point B? What if, hidden within the congestion and the honking horns, we could uncover a pathway to mindfulness, resilience, and even gratitude?

Road Rage to Road Sage: 10 Lessons You Can Learn in LA Gridlock invites you to reimagine the way you experience your commute. Instead of viewing traffic as an unfortunate barrier to your day, think of it as an unexpected teacher. Every red light, every lane change, every unexpected detour holds a lesson—a chance to practice patience, embrace acceptance, or show kindness. These lessons may be subtle, hidden beneath the surface of everyday frustrations, but they're there if we choose to look. And in recognizing these small spiritual teachings, we can transform our time on the road into something infinitely more valuable.

This book isn't a guide on how to avoid traffic or make it go faster, nor is it a traditional spiritual manual. Rather, it's an invitation to find meaning and presence in the most mundane of circumstances. Each chapter explores a specific lesson drawn from the daily experience of driving —whether it's the power of breathing to calm road rage, the practice of gratitude amidst the honks and hustle, or the surprising impact of small acts of kindness on our emotional well-being.

The chapters are laid out into three sections, beginning with the introduction of a typical traffic trial and its potential transcendental truth, laying the foundation for reflection and further exploration. In the next chapter segment, we illustrate these ideas with real-life examples—drawing from my own experiences as well as those of friends and family—to provide relatable, practical insights.

And finally, in the third segment, I'm calling "The Rearview", we check that proverbial 20/20 hindsight to get a view of the bigger picture from a few different perspectives, and maybe find one or two nuggets of wisdom that we can take with us down the road.

One more thing; feel free to take your time with

this. The book is structured as a chapter a day read, allowing time to consider and reflect on the lessons contained within each of the chapters.

You don't need a quiet meditation retreat to discover the path to inner peace. Sometimes, enlightenment arrives while crawling along on the 101 Hollywood Freeway. And as you journey through these pages, you may just find that, despite the gridlock, you are already exactly where you're meant to be.

Let's take this journey together, one mile at a time.

CHAPTER ONE

Patience In Gridlock

"Patience is not simply the ability to wait - it's how we behave while we're waiting."
—Joyce Meyer

Interstate 405, aka the San Diego Freeway, is the main north/south artery for the Westside of L.A. and roughly follows the outline of the Pacific coast. The 405 is one of the busiest freeways in the country, the most commonly used highway to LAX, and a bypass for I-5.

Now imagine you're stuck on the I-405 freeway during rush hour, surrounded by a sea of brake lights. Your destination seems miles away, and the frustration builds with every passing minute. But what if this gridlock is offering you the opportunity to practice the art of patience?

Patience isn't merely the ability to wait; it's how we behave while waiting. Traffic jams provide a unique space to practice patience and learn to let go of the need for instant gratification. Instead of allowing anger and frustration to take over, we can choose to accept the situation as it is, realizing that our irritation won't change the outcome.

In these moments, patience becomes a spiritual practice. By embracing the slow pace, you can start to notice things you might otherwise miss – the beauty of the sunset, the rhythm of your breathing, or even the quiet hum of your car. These observations can transform a frustrating experience into a meditative one, where you learn to find peace amidst chaos. Patience in gridlock teaches us that sometimes, slowing down is exactly what we need to truly appreciate the journey.

Patience Takes Practice

"It was a weekday afternoon in Los Angeles, and I had just left the set of a small movie I'd been working on all week with dreams of a quick escape to the beach. As I merged onto the infamous 405, I felt confident—probably overly so. The afternoon sun was shining, so I cracked the windows to enjoy the breeze. I was certain I'd get to MB (Manhattan Beach) before the crowds, find a great parking spot, and sink my feet into the sand with my friend Lisa, cocktails in hand, before the golden hour. But of course, the 405 had other plans.

Almost as soon as I hit the on-ramp, I found myself crawling into the sort of bumper-to-bumper traffic that only a seasoned Angeleno could properly loathe. The type of seething hostility that includes a healthy portion of self-hatred for knowing better. A rookie mistake, getting on here during rush hour!

We're inching forward, eyes darting between the speedometer reading zero and the clock ticking away with every passing minute. Frustration began to bubble up. The beach was getting farther away in my mind as the line of brake lights stretched before me in an endless, fiery sea.

I glanced at the dashboard clock. 5:45 p.m. By now, I had moved exactly... 200 feet. I tried flipping through radio stations, but all of them were covering different flavors of the same traffic report. The dreaded CIG (pronounced "sig") alert! Apparently, my hopes for a breezy drive had been a bit too optimistic.

This wasn't traffic; it was a parking lot, a commuter's worst nightmare. With nowhere to go and nothing to do, I felt a familiar restlessness creep in. I checked my phone to see if I could call anyone for a chat, only to find that I had drained my battery down to 3% from a full day's use. And of course! no charger cable.

For a few minutes, I sat there festering. I fumed. I think I even banged my fists on the steering wheel for dramatic effect, though the only one to witness this display was the Bev Hills hottie in the black SUV to my left. I was stuck, plain and simple.

But then a thought floated up, almost like a whisper: What if you just... accepted it? While the thought was not alien to me, it certainly was not an innate instinct of mine either. I practically laughed out loud at the thought. But there was an undeniable logic to it. I was here, stuck on the 405, and no amount of rage was going to part the sea of cars. I was literally going nowhere fast and I'd left my Jetsen car in the rooftop garage.

So, I took a deep breath. And then another. I closed

my eyes for a moment—just a second or two, don't worry—and tried something different: relaxation. Just for a minute, I leaned back in my comfy leather bucket seat and let the engine's low growl wash over me. The sound of a car honking a couple lanes over seemed a little less irritating and more like background noise. I focused on loosening my white-knuckle grip on the steering wheel.

It felt strange at first, but surprisingly, my body started to settle. I caught myself easing into the stillness. Rather than scanning the road for nonexistent openings, I let my gaze wander. To my left was now a golden haired Afghan Hound poking its head out the backseat window of the Bev Hills SUV, tongue hanging out, oblivious and unconcerned. The car on my right had a bumper sticker that read, "Not All Who Wander Are Lost"—a painfully appropriate sentiment. I became aware of the colors of the brake lights ahead of me. They held a nostalgic beauty as the red and blood orange hues seemed to reflect the evening light.

In this state of surrender, I found myself letting go of expectations and accepting the reality of the moment. I allowed my thoughts to drift, reflecting on how recently I tended to approach other areas of my life with the same rigid, single-minded focus. How often did I try to force things to go my way, instead of simply adjusting to the way things were?

I lost track of time a bit, which was a nice change

from my usual anxious clock-watching. Eventually, the traffic began to ease—though I had almost forgotten where I was trying to go. When we started moving again, I felt no surge of relief, no rush to speed ahead. Instead, I eased onto the gas pedal with a strange calm, moving forward with everyone else.

It was twighlight by the time I reached the beach. Parking was a challenge, but it didn't bother me. I grabbed a spot a few blocks away and walked, enjoying the cool air and the fading sun. There was something comforting in realizing that I had weathered the chaos without losing my cool. I had made it, after all, and the journey had been far more interesting when I stopped fighting it.

Now, whenever I find myself trapped in another one of LA's infamous traffic jams, or even an equally infamous Costco checkout line, I remember that day. I remind myself to breathe, to look around, and to surrender to the situation, however inconvenient it might seem. Patience is a practice, and the road —like life—is as good a place as any to start practicing."   – James WH

The Rearview

Clearly patience is not just a passive act; it's an active choice that empowers us to respond to challenges with grace. When stuck in traffic, we often feel helpless and frustrated, but these moments are an opportunity to shift our perspective. By accepting the situation and letting go of control, we create space for mindfulness, self-reflection, and growth.

In many spiritual traditions, surrender is a form of strength. The Taoist principle of *wu wei* (literally, doing nothing) teaches us to align with the flow of life rather than fight against it. In traffic, this might mean reframing delays as opportunities to practice stillness and presence.

Cognitive behavioral psychology shows us that how we interpret a situation influences our emotional response. Instead of viewing traffic as a waste of time, try reframing it as a chance to build emotional resilience, and deepen our connection to the present. This small shift in perspective can transform frustration into calm acceptance.

The Stoics believed in focusing on what we can control and accepting what we cannot. Marcus Aurelius wrote, *"You have power over your mind—not outside events. Realize this, and you will find strength."* In traffic, you can't control the flow of cars, but you can control your response.

JAMES WILDERHANCOCK

Suggested reading: *Wherever You Go, There You Are: Mindfulness Meditation in Everyday Life* by Jon Kabat-Zinn

CHAPTER TWO

Finding Joy In The Journey

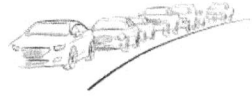

"It is good to have an end to journey toward, but it is the journey that matters in the end."
– Ursula K. Le Guin

In a city where getting from point A to point B, C then D can be a challenge, it's easy to focus solely on the destination. But what if we shifted our focus to finding joy in the journey itself? Whether it's listening to your favorite music, an engaging podcast, learning a new language, or simply enjoying the scenery, there are many ways to make the most of your time in traffic.

Finding joy in the journey teaches us to appreciate the present moment, no matter the circumstances. It's a reminder that life is not just about reaching our goals, but about experiencing and enjoying the process along the way. By seeking out and savoring small moments of joy, we can turn even the most mundane commute into a source of happiness and fulfillment.

Taking The Scenic Route

"It was a Saturday, and I had plans to meet a friend for brunch across town. Los Angeles is one of those places where "across town" can mean anything from a quick 20 minutes to a staggering two-hour crawl, depending on the whims of the traffic gods. Today, I was headed to Sherman Oaks- The Valley- and it seemed they were in a particularly mischievous mood. The navigation app estimated a 45-minute drive from my current location in Pasadena, but as I merged onto the 110 the ETA kept climbing. Red lines were snaking across the map, roadblocks appeared out of nowhere, and I could practically feel my stress meter rising with every passing minute.

My friend texted me, "Stuck in traffic?" Yes, she knew me well. "Take the scenic route instead—it's a beautiful day!" Now, I normally don't stray from the fastest route. Efficient driving was my bread and butter. But staring at the gridlock in front of me, I thought, why not? I exited the freeway and found myself on Mulholland Drive, famous for its twisting, turning path through the hills, its panoramic views, and, of course, its sharp hairpin turns that made it feel like a joyride from the movies. Especially in my new 2013 Fiat Abarth!

The second I turned onto Mulholland, my whole mood shifted. Gone were the impatient honks and frustrated faces; instead, there was a winding road stretched out before me, dotted with pullouts for scenic views and the occasional bold cyclist. I rolled down the windows, letting the warm breeze fill the car as I made my way through the curves. Driving through this unexpected detour felt like stepping into another world, one where rush and efficiency had no place. Suddenly I was in love with SoCal again.

As I drove, I noticed details I had somehow

forgotten in my years in L.A. On my left, the city sprawled out endlessly, skyscrapers poking into the blue sky. To my right, the hills were lush and green, dusted with wildflowers. I pulled over at a viewpoint, one of those spots where, on a clear day, you can see all the way to the ocean. I stood there for a moment, taking in the whole city laid out like a mosaic, feeling both wonderfully small and incredibly lucky to be right there.

Back in the car, I continued at a leisurely pace. At one point, a car zipped past, its driver clearly in a hurry to get somewhere. I would have done the same 30 minutes ago, but now I found myself chuckling, almost pitying them for missing out on the drive itself. What was my rush? My friend would wait, and besides, the journey was turning out to be a highlight of my day, with 311's *Stereolithic* providing the perfect soundtrack.

As I slowed around a curve, I passed a group of hikers at a trailhead, excitedly heading up the path. Seeing their eagerness reminded me of the days I used to hike these hills myself, back when I first came to Los Angeles and everything felt like an adventure. It struck me then that there was something profoundly peaceful about simply taking your time—whether on a trail or a winding road. I had set out to reach a brunch, but the journey was filling me up in a way I hadn't anticipated.

When I finally reached Beverly Glen Boulevard and

the end of my Mulholland adventure, I felt like I had been transported, not just across town, but out of my usual world of routines and rushes. My friend greeted me with a smirk as I arrived, almost an hour late, but all I could do was laugh and tell her about my unplanned adventure. Brunch was delicious, but it wasn't the best part of the day. That honor went to the drive itself.

Now, whenever I'm stuck in traffic or find myself itching to just get somewhere already, I remember that detour. I remember the joy of winding roads, of taking time and truly noticing my surroundings. It's not just about getting from A to B. Sometimes, the journey holds treasures you never expected, if only you're willing to slow down and look for them. And maybe—just maybe—that's worth being late for."
– James WH

The Rearview

The Taoist principle of ziran, meaning "naturalness" or "spontaneity," beautifully aligns with this experience. Ziran emphasizes living in harmony with the natural flow of life, embracing situations as they arise, and letting things unfold without forced control.

When I chose to leave the congested freeway and meander along Mulholland Drive, I stepped into ziran. Rather than resisting the traffic or clinging to rigid plans, I allowed myself to flow with the moment, adapting to the circumstances with ease and openness. This spontaneous decision mirrors the Taoist ideal of aligning oneself with life's rhythms instead of fighting against them.

The unfolding beauty of Mulholland Dr.—its curves, vistas, and peaceful ambiance—became a reflection of ziran in action. By releasing the need for efficiency and perfection, we create space to appreciate the natural spontaneity of the journey, finding joy and wisdom in an unexpected detour. This practice of embracing what comes naturally, without undue resistance or attachment, is at the heart of Taoist living.

We learn that when we trust in the natural order, the path itself provides the lessons and experiences we need, often revealing treasures far beyond what we might have planned. Taking the scenic route was more than a physical detour—it became a spiritual practice, a way of living in alignment with the Tao.

Neuroscience underscores this idea as well, revealing that novelty and curiosity activate the brain's reward system, making experiences like a spontaneous drive feel invigorating and meaningful. Each curve of the road and new vista reigniting appreciation for the city I'd grown accustomed to.

The next time you face an unexpected detour—whether in traffic or life—remember that the journey itself can be an adventure. Slow down, roll down the windows, and let the fresh air remind you to savor the ride. The treasures you discover might just change your day—or even your outlook on life.

Suggested reading: *Be Here Now* by Ram Das

CHAPTER THREE

The Power Of Breath

*"Feelings come and go like clouds in a windy sky.
Conscious breathing is my anchor."*
– Thich Nhat Hanh

Traffic can be a source of immense stress, leading to tension, anxiety and even illness. One powerful tool to combat this is conscious breathing. When you find yourself stuck in traffic, take a few deep breaths. Inhale deeply through your nose, hold for a moment, and exhale slowly through your mouth. This simple practice can help calm your nervous system, reduce stress, and bring you back to the present moment.

The power of breath is a fundamental spiritual practice that can be applied in many areas of life. By focusing on your breath, you can create a sense of inner peace and balance, no matter what external circumstances you face. In traffic, as in life, taking a moment to breathe can make all the difference in how you experience the world around you.

Finding Calm In The Daily Storm

"It was a typical weekday early morning set call, and I was running late. It was raining, my tea was lukewarm and even my Deva Premal playlist wasn't helping my mood.

Traffic was moving slower than my year-old locally sourced honey this morning. As I inched along the freeway, the anxiety and worry that had started as a low hum in my chest began building into a full-blown internal symphony. I hate being late to set and every brake light I saw was like a mini jolt of adrenaline. Each minute that passed made me clench Arabella's steering wheel a little harder.

I tried flipping through radio stations, running through my mental list of calming mantras, and even took a swig of my cold green tea, but nothing seemed to settle the nerves. It was then, mid-traffic frenzy, that I remembered something I'd learned at a retreat the year before. Just a few deep, intentional breaths might be enough to help calm my racing mind. Well, I thought, might as well try. Nothing else was working.

So, I took my first breath. I breathed in slowly, filling my lungs completely, and exhaled just as slowly, trying to let go of some of the tension I always held in my shoulders. Then I took another deep breath, in and out. On the third breath, I felt a slight shift, like the fog of frustration was starting to clear. I decided to keep going, focusing all my attention on each inhale and exhale, letting myself settle into the simple rhythm of breathing. For a moment, my mind stopped dwelling on the traffic jam, the clock, and the crew call I'd be late for. All that existed was the steady flow of air in and out.

By the fifth or sixth breath, something strange happened—I felt calm–and in that calmness the hum of engines, the rhythmic slapping of windshield wipers, even the soft drone of my heater suddenly felt calming. My car, my small, idling space on the road, became an unexpected refuge from the chaos around me.

And then, as if on cue, I spotted a driver in the next lane over, clearly going through his own Monday-morning struggle. He was gripping the wheel, his face set in a tight grimace, likely on his third cup of coffee and wishing he was anywhere but here. For the first time, instead of reacting with irritation, I felt a wave of empathy. He was caught in the same web of tension that I had been only moments before, likely unaware that he, too, had an immediate tool at his disposal. It was just breathing, after all—something we do without thinking about 22 thousand times a day. But in traffic, here and now, I realized it could transform my experience.

Over the next several minutes, I continued my practice. Whenever I felt my worry spike, I took another deep breath. Instead of seeing red lights as impediments, I began to see them as reminders to breathe, little invitations to pause and let go of my tension. I even sang a little Mac Davis. Soon, I found myself approaching the situation differently. Every few moments, I'd look out at the sea of cars around me and think, "We're all in this together." Everyone was just trying to get somewhere, doing their best, feeling the weight of the wait. This realization brought me a level of peace I hadn't expected to feel—certainly not on a jam-packed freeway.

When traffic eventually started to move again, I noticed I was in no rush to speed up. The breathwork had worked a kind of magic. I arrived at my destination calmer, more present, and without the usual post-commute irritability.

That day taught me a powerful lesson about the benefits of breath, not just for coping with traffic, but for finding peace in any challenging situation. Since then, every time I'm caught in a traffic jam or start feeling impatient, I take a few deep breaths. It doesn't change the traffic, but it changes me, and sometimes, that's all you really need." *–James WH*

The Rearview

In moments of stress, we often forget that the simplest tools can offer the most profound relief. The power of breath, often taken for granted, has the ability to transform our internal AND external experience. As we rush through life, fixated on the end goal, we frequently overlook the present moment—the one place where we have the ability to find peace.

Yogis have long recognized the transformative

power of breathwork, using it as a tool to achieve various states of mental, physical, and spiritual well-being. In practices like *pranayama*, which is the Sanskrit term for "control of the breath," yogis intentionally manipulate their breath to influence the body's energy, calm the nervous system, and bring focus to the present moment.

One of the most common breathwork practices in yoga is *ujjayi breath*, also known as "victorious breath." This technique involves gently constricting the back of the throat to create a soft, whispering sound as you breathe in and out. The rhythmic nature of ujjayi breath not only helps to focus the mind but also activates the parasympathetic nervous system, promoting relaxation and reducing the stress response.

In his book *The Relaxation Response*, Dr. Herbert Benson explains how deep, mindful breathing can activate this response, providing immediate relief from anxiety. This can be incredibly useful during moments of frustration or anxiety. By focusing on the sound and rhythm of the breath, one can shift the focus from external tension to internal peace, using the breath as an anchor.

Another common technique is *nadi shodhana*, or alternate nostril breathing. (Appendix A) This practice balances the two hemispheres of the brain, calming the mind and promoting mental clarity. It is often used in yoga to prepare the practitioner for meditation or to clear any mental blockages. In a stressful situation like traffic, using alternate nostril breathing can help reduce the mental clutter and foster a sense of balance, allowing us to approach the experience with a clearer mind and a calmer heart.

In more advanced practices, yogis use breathwork to guide themselves into deeper states of consciousness. *Kundalini yoga*, for instance, incorporates intense breathwork techniques like *breath of fire* (rapid, rhythmic breathing through the nose) to awaken and elevate energy within the body, encouraging heightened awareness and spiritual growth. Although Kundalini techniques are more advanced, the principle behind them—the power of breath to shape consciousness—is a powerful concept that can be adapted for any situation, from meditation to navigating rush hour traffic.

Suggested Reading: *The Science of Breath* by Swami Rama, Alan Hymes, Rudolph M. Ballentine

CHAPTER FOUR

Listening To Inner Guidance

"The only real valuable thing is intuition."
– Albert Einstein

Navigating the busy streets of L.A. often involves making quick decisions – which route to take, when to change lanes, or whether to detour. In these moments, listening to your intuition can be incredibly valuable. Sometimes, a gut feeling or an inner voice will guide you to take a different route, avoiding potential delays or hazards.

Listening to inner guidance is a practice that extends beyond driving. It's about trusting your instincts and tuning into your inner wisdom. By paying attention to these subtle cues, you can navigate not only the roads but also the journey of life with greater ease and confidence. Trusting yourself and your inner guidance can lead to more harmonious and fulfilling experiences.

Use The Force Dude

"It was one of those summer days when life seemed to conspire to remind you of its unpredictability. My car was in the shop—again. It was an old beater, the kind you affectionately call "'ole reliable" only because it mostly gets you where you're going. Today, it was taking a break, so my mom graciously volunteered to drive me to a job interview across town. The plan was simple: make it to the interview, and then, job or no job, treat ourselves to lunch at a favorite spot that we didn't often visit due to the distance. The interview was as much an excuse for the outing as it was a career opportunity.

Traffic was its usual weekday chaos—cars jockeying for position, work trucks hauling equipment, delivery vans zipping by. Among the sea of vehicles, one caught my eye: an oversized Ford pickup hauling a long extension ladder perched precariously on what looked like a makeshift speed-rail rack in the truck bed. Something about it made me uneasy. Maybe it was how the ladder shifted slightly with every bump, or how the truck seemed to appear alongside us at every standstill, like an ominous side character in a road movie. We stopped for gas and drinks at one point, and there it was again, looming in the background like the villainous semi from Duel. I told myself it was just a weird coincidence.

Back on the road, I was doing my best to ignore the truck, trying to focus on the hopeful idea of a post-interview celebration. But the truck was hard to ignore when it pulled into the fast lane ahead of us, ladder swaying dangerously. That's when it hit me— a gut feeling, a sharp, inexplicable certainty.

I turned to my mom, urgency spilling into my

voice. "Get out of this lane. Now."

She didn't hesitate. Whether it was my tone or some instinct of her own kicking in, she veered right into the next lane without argument. The timing was uncanny. Barely a second after we moved, the ladder shot out of the truck bed like a missile, hurtling past the driver's side of our car with terrifying speed. It could have smashed into the windshield, or worse, torn straight through it. Instead, it sailed harmlessly down the road, clattering to a stop behind us.

Silence filled the car, the kind that follows a brush with disaster. My mom finally broke it. "How did you know?" she asked, her voice steady but quiet.

I shrugged, not sure how to answer. "I just... knew," I said, though that hardly explained it. It wasn't logic or observation that told me to move. It was something deeper, a visceral, unshakable pull, like a voice speaking from somewhere beyond reason.

Intuition, gut feeling, "Spidey-Sense" —whatever you call it, that instinct saved us that day. And though I didn't understand how or why it worked, I was profoundly grateful that I'd listened. If I'd brushed it off as paranoia or coincidence, the outcome could have been very different.

That day taught me the importance of tuning into that inner guidance, of trusting the voice that doesn't speak with words but with a clarity you can feel in your bones. Sometimes it's a whisper, sometimes a shout, but when it speaks, it's worth listening. Whether it's deciding to switch lanes or choosing a path in life, intuition has a way of steering us toward safety—or opportunity—if we let it.

As we drove on, my mom and I exchanged knowing glances, the weight of what had just happened settling between us. We didn't need to say much. We both understood the gravity of the near-miss, and we both knew it was a reminder to trust the unexplainable. When we finally made it to the interview and later to that long-anticipated lunch, I couldn't help but reflect on the experience. It wasn't just a lesson in road safety; it was a lesson in listening—to the world, to the moment, and most importantly, to that quiet, guiding voice inside."
– Michael K.

The Rearview

Intuition has long been regarded as a spiritual and extra-sensory gift across many traditions, often viewed as an inner compass guiding us toward the right decisions, even when we don't fully understand how we arrived at them. In spiritual practices, intuition is believed to be an alignment with deeper, universal truths that transcend our logical minds.

In many indigenous cultures, for example, intuition is closely linked to ancestral knowledge, a way of perceiving the world that draws from collective wisdom passed down through generations. This is echoed in practices like shamanism, where intuition is seen as a way of tapping into unseen realms—whether that be the spirit world, the collective unconscious, or the energetic flow of nature. Shamans often claim that intuition connects us with non-ordinary reality, where messages and insights are received through dreams, visions, and subtle impressions.

In Hinduism, particularly within the yogic traditions, intuition is considered a function of the *ajna* or third eye chakra, which is said to govern higher consciousness and the ability to perceive beyond ordinary perception. The practice of meditation is used to heighten this intuitive sense, with the belief that true insight comes from aligning with the divine and the universal flow of energy, known as *prana*. This yogic philosophy teaches that intuition, like breath, is an innate, natural force that we can cultivate by quieting the mind and tuning into the subtle frequencies around us.

Similarly, in Western spiritual traditions, intuition is often regarded as a form of divine guidance. Mystics and saints through history, such as St. Teresa of Ávila or St. John of the Cross, spoke of "the inner voice" or "the still, small voice" as an essential way to receive God's direction. This is not just intellectual knowledge, but a deep, knowing awareness that transcends the ego and taps into the divine.

Even science has studied so-called "extrasensory perception" (ESP) phenomena such as clairvoyance, telepathy, and precognition- often associated with heightened intuition in both modern metaphysical practices and ancient traditions. Research into ESP suggests that human beings have abilities to pick up on information beyond the five senses, an idea that is supported by concepts in quantum physics and the collective unconscious. Carl Jung, the Swiss psychiatrist, psychotherapist and psychologist who founded the school of analytical psychology, argued that synchronicities—meaningful coincidences—are manifestations of the unconscious mind linking us to a greater, unseen order in the universe. In his work, Jung proposed that intuition plays a key role in allowing us to access these synchronicities, seeing patterns in seemingly random events.

Thus, intuition is not only about responding to physical cues but also about tapping into an interconnected web of knowledge and awareness that extends far beyond the immediate moment.

Whether through a quiet whisper in the heart, a sudden knowing, or the recognition of unseen connections, intuition is a universal tool—one that, when trusted, can guide us safely through life's uncertainties.

Suggested reading: *Intuition for Starters: How to Know and Trust Your Inner Guidance* by Swami Kriyananda

CHAPTER FIVE

Letting Go Of Anger

"Holding on to anger is like drinking poison and expecting the other person to die."
– Buddha

R oad rage is an all too common experience in modern traffic, but it rarely serves us. Holding onto anger can harm our mental and physical well-being. Learning to let go of anger and respond to frustrating situations with calm and understanding is a valuable spiritual practice.

Letting go of anger in traffic teaches us to cultivate emotional intelligence and self-control. It reminds us that we have the power to choose our reactions and that responding with anger only perpetuates negativity. By letting go of anger, we can create a more peaceful and harmonious experience for ourselves and those around us.

Transforming Rage Into Reflection

"It was 2014, and I had a crack-of-dawn TSA appointment at LAX to get my travel certificate. I needed to drive from the San Fernando Valley—basically Burbank–only a few blocks from Stoopid Buddy Stoodios, which, hilariously, had offered me a job the minute I announced I was leaving town. Funny, right? (Author's note: It is an unwritten Hollywood rule that you will be offered work every time you try to leave town.)

With a 7:45 a.m. appointment on the books, I

had dutifully set my alarm early and was whipping up some coffee and oatmeal while I gave Google Maps a quick check at 6:30. Forty-five minutes to LAX, it said. Perfect! I figured if I left by 6:45, I'd be golden. So, with my documents in hand and my determination at an all-time high, I was in the car by 6:47, cruising down Ventura Freeway toward the 405 like a modern road warrior.

And then, bam—out of nowhere, I see the color creeping across my map screen. At first, it's the regular yellow indicating "slowing traffic." That would change quickly. Soon, the whole map is drowning in a godforsaken blood-red hue as far as I can scroll, from my car all the way to LAX and everywhere in between. It's like the city of angels had finally fallen into Dante's tenth circle: eternal bumper-to-bumper purgatory.

Okay, deep breath. I'm stuck, but maybe I can let TSA know I'm running late. So I call, get their voicemail, and leave a message. Five messages, actually, as I inched along, one car length at a time, hoping maybe they'd miraculously squeeze me in when I arrived…sometime around sunset.

After an hour of soul-crushing inching, my frustration peaked. I'm gripping the steering wheel, screaming internally (and a little externally). The entire day's plan is evaporating in front of me, and all I can do is crawl along with the rest of LA's hopeless masses, trying to get somewhere—

anywhere.

Eventually, the rage burst out of me. I'm beating the steering wheel, letting it all go, only to realize that, weirdly, I actually felt a bit better afterward. Rage drained, I ducked out of the far left lane, slowly shifting one lane at a time to the right, waving my thanks to anyone who let me over. I found an offramp, swerved down a side street, pulled over, and, with one last primal scream at the dashboard and a little crying, admitted defeat. Today, TSA was not in the cards.

On that day something clicked. That awful mix of helpless rage and claustrophobic frustration? It actually shifted something in me. Maybe it's what people mean by "learning to let go." Or maybe it's a kind of DIY Zen therapy courtesy of L.A.'s notoriously cursed freeways. Either way, I'm back in Portland now, and the traffic here is beginning to morph into something vaguely L.A.-esque, but I've got a new mindset on my side. Whenever I start feeling the old road rage brewing, I remember that day on the 405, trying to get to LAX, shouting at the universe. Now, I realize the universe wasn't actually against me.

Funny how things work. I mean, don't get me wrong—I'm not some saint who floats above gridlock with a beatific smile. I have been having rage issues for all of my life but this experience on the 405 has changed me. I don't know if this is a Zen thing or just aversion therapy but there's something liberating in realizing there's nothing you can do. Sometimes, you just have to sit back, breathe deep, and let the traffic gods have the last laugh." – *Ian B.*

The Rearview

In the aftermath of that infuriating traffic debacle, the experience became a poignant lesson in letting go of anger for my friend Ian. Psychologically, we know that holding on to anger can be detrimental to our mental and physical well-being. Research in emotional regulation supports the idea that repressing or nurturing anger only exacerbates stress, leading to both short-term and long-term health problems. The act of releasing it, as Ian did that day on the 405, was a form of emotional catharsis—a psychological release that temporarily freed him from the grip of frustration.

From a spiritual perspective, letting go of anger is emphasized in many traditions. In Buddhism, practitioners are encouraged to observe emotions as they arise, but without becoming attached to, or identifying with them. This process is known as *vipassana* or "insight meditation", where they cultivate a deep awareness of the present moment, including their thoughts, feelings, and physical sensations. The key to this practice is *non-identification*—recognizing that emotions, thoughts, and experiences are transient and not inherently part of who we are. By observing them without attachment, we prevent ourselves from becoming overwhelmed or defined by them.

The *Satipatthana Sutta*, one of the central teachings on mindfulness in Buddhism, outlines this process of awareness and non-attachment. It teaches practitioners to observe not only their physical sensations but also their emotional and mental states, cultivating a compassionate and non-judgmental awareness. By practicing mindfulness in this way, we begin to see that emotions, like all phenomena, arise and pass away, and that they do not define our true nature.

Psychologically, this approach can be understood through the lens of *cognitive defusion*, a concept explored in Acceptance and Commitment Therapy (ACT). Cognitive defusion teaches that we are not our thoughts or emotions, but simply the observer of them. Sound Familiar?

By practicing awareness, we can see and detach from our emotional responses, which allows us to make more thoughtful, intentional decisions rather than reacting automatically from a place of anger or distress.

Similarly, Stoicism, which focuses on controlling

our reactions to external events, also teaches that anger is a natural response to external frustrations, but it is our choice whether we allow it to control us. The practice of *apatheia* (freedom from passion) refers to a state of being free from emotional disturbance and irrational passions. This philosophy highlights the power of shifting our mindset to accept the things we cannot change, allowing us to move forward with greater peace and equanimity.

Suggested reading: *A Gentle Answer: Our 'Secret Weapon' in an Age of Us Against Them* by Scott Sauls

CHAPTER SIX

Letting Go Of Judgment

"When you judge another, you do not define them, you define yourself."
– Wayne Dyer

Driving through the diverse neighborhoods of Los Angeles, such as Downtown, Hollywood, and West Hollywood, you'll inevitably encounter a wide array of people and situations. You might see individuals who appear unusual or homeless, and it's easy to form quick judgments based on their appearance or behavior. However, these moments offer a powerful lesson in letting go of judgment and embracing compassion.

Every person has a story, and the outward appearances we observe from our car windows only scratch the surface. The individual wearing tattered clothes or carrying all their belongings in a shopping cart has a rich, complex life that we cannot fully understand from a glance. Letting go of judgment means recognizing that we do not know the full extent of someone's circumstances. It's about shifting from a mindset of criticism to one of empathy and understanding.

Instead of reacting with discomfort or disdain, use these encounters as opportunities to practice kindness and open-mindedness. Acknowledge that every person is doing the best they can with the resources they have. This shift in perspective can deepen your sense of connection and humanity. By letting go of judgment, you allow yourself to see the inherent worth and dignity in every individual, fostering a more compassionate and inclusive worldview.

Judgement vibrates at a very low frequency. Letting go of judgment extends beyond traffic encounters; it's a spiritual practice that can transform your interactions and relationships. It encourages you to approach others with curiosity rather than criticism, creating space for genuine connection and empathy. In a city as vibrant and diverse as Los Angeles, this practice is not only beneficial but essential for fostering a more harmonious and compassionate community.

A Life-Altering Traffic Jam

"I was on my way to an interview for a house manager position at the estate of the founder of Milton's Crackers in Rancho Santa Fe. A job like this was my dream — I'd be managing a beautiful estate, working with animals, and living the sort of life that seemed out of reach until now. I'd been told the owner was extremely busy, with another appointment right after our meeting, so I couldn't afford to be late. But as I inched along the 405, frustration boiled up. Gridlock had turned into a near standstill, and I had no idea why.

I was already stewing over being behind schedule when we hit another complete stop. I looked around, sighing heavily, wondering what had caused this nightmare traffic jam. Then, as I finally reached the accident scene, I saw a crumpled motorcycle lying on the side of the road and a blue tarp covering what could only be a person. In that moment, my anger vanished, replaced by a wave of guilt and sadness. I'd been furious over the possibility of missing out on a job interview, yet someone else's life had just ended. This stranger was never going home that night, never seeing loved ones again, and I was mad about a career opportunity?

That moment put things in perspective. We tend to judge situations on how they affect us, losing sight of the bigger picture. I was ready to label that gridlock as a "nuisance" and complain about my day without thinking there could be real human loss behind it. I'd spent so much energy judging the situation by how it impacted me that I didn't consider how anyone else might have been affected until it was staring me in the face.

Missing that interview stung, but it led me to a path I might never have taken otherwise. I ended up in the film industry, something I hadn't even considered then, and eventually found a whole new direction for my life. We can judge moments quickly, labeling them as obstacles or inconveniences, but sometimes what feels like a detour might be setting us on the right course.

In the end, letting go of our snap judgments

can help us see situations for what they are, and maybe even help us recognize that our paths don't always go as planned but still lead us somewhere meaningful." — *Krysta K.*

The Rearview

Judgment is often a reaction to how we interpret the world around us. In the case of the traffic jam that literally detoured Krysta's life, it was easy to fall into the trap of labeling the situation as bad luck, with all the frustration that comes with it. But as soon as the reality of a life lost became clear, her judgment dissolved. This shift highlights an essential insight from both spiritual and psychological practices.

This shift reflects principles found in *Taoism* which teaches that the judgments we make about events often lead to resistance or conflict with the inherent flow of life. The Taoist concept of *wu wei*—or "effortless action"—encourages us to release the impulse to judge or control circumstances. Instead, we are urged to accept what is, acknowledging that things unfold as they should, even when they seem inconvenient or painful in the moment.

The philosopher Laozi (Lao Tzu), who is credited with the foundational texts of Taoism, said, *"The more laws and order are made prominent, the more thieves and robbers there will be."* In other words, when we cling to rigid judgments or try to impose our expectations on situations, we create disharmony. By letting go of judgment, we begin to move with the flow of life, much like water finding its way around obstacles, adjusting to the environment, and ultimately creating its own path.

Psychologically, the practice of non-judgment can be linked to *cognitive flexibility*, the ability to adapt our thinking to new situations and insights. Research in this field suggests that when we release the need for black-and-white (good or bad) thinking, we become more resilient and less overwhelmed by life's unpredictability. In doing so, we foster greater emotional well-being, as we are no longer bound by preconceived notions or judgments that can lead to frustration.

Taoism and psychological research both highlight the power of letting go of rigid judgments as a way to embrace life's inherent uncertainty and find peace. In the case of the traffic jam, allowing the moment to unfold without judgment not only provided clarity but also led to an unexpected realization about life's detours—sometimes, what we initially resist can ultimately guide us toward new, meaningful paths.

Suggested reading: *The Art of Happiness* by Dalai Lama and Howard Cutler

CHAPTER SEVEN

Learning From Mistakes

"The only real mistake is the one from which we learn nothing."
– Henry Ford

We all know that sinking feeling when we see the bright red and blue lights in our rearview. Receiving a speeding or parking ticket can be frustrating and inconvenient, often leading to feelings of annoyance, fear or anger. However, these moments offer an opportunity to reflect on our actions and learn from our mistakes. A ticket serves as a reminder to slow down, pay attention, and follow the rules designed to keep everyone safe.

Making mistakes is part of the human condition. "To err is human", right? But it is also a fundamental component of evolution. The key is to learn from them and make better choices moving forward. A speeding ticket may teach us the importance of being mindful of our speed and surroundings, while a parking ticket can remind us to be more attentive to signs and our surroundings. Instead of dwelling on the inconvenience, we can use these experiences as lessons in personal responsibility and growth.

Without Mistakes, There Is No Growth

"My own humbling experience came on an evening when I was cruising back into LA after a few years away on a job in Portland. This was the end of a beautiful four day drive via Eastern Oregon, Utah and Arizona which included a side trip to Area 51 and a spontaneous concert in downtown Tucson with the late, great Sharon Jones and the Dap Tones. These last few miles on the I-5 to the 134 into Burbank was all that was between me and a warm bed.

Traffic was light and my foot was heavy on Arabella's gas pedal. This was the first long-distance road trip for my new Fiat Abarth and I had been enjoying every bit of her speed and agility on the road. Maybe a wee bit too much now as I rolled into town. Just as I was within two miles of my exit, I heard the unmistakable sound of a siren and saw the flash of red and blue lights in my rearview mirror. Ugh! Cue gut drop.

The officer, who couldn't have looked more disapproving if he tried, calmly explained the importance of speed limits and responsible driving as I fumbled for my license and registration- embarrassment and frustration mingling within me. Here I was, 1600 miles of trouble free road warrioring behind me and I get pulled over within sight of the finish line. The ticket, it turned out, was hefty—a significant blow to my wallet and a major check on my driving record. I was moving pretty fast.

But what bothered me most wasn't the fine or even my record—it was the nagging sense of self-reproach. Why had I been so absent minded? Why had I literally ignored the signs just to make it home a little bit faster? In my rush, I'd fallen into the classic trap of trying to save time by rushing, only to end up losing more time than if I'd simply been patient and cautious.

After the encounter, as I drove on, my frustration slowly transformed into reflection. In my everyday life, how often had I let impatience get the better of me?

My actions that evening represented a mindset that I didn't want to carry forward. Mistakes are often painted in a negative light, but they're also our greatest teachers, as they hold up a mirror to our habits and tendencies. This was a moment for me to recognize that my own rushing and corner-cutting was not only ineffective but was creating stress and inviting preventable problems . The ticket was a costly reminder, but it was also a valuable one.

In the days that followed, I found myself approaching my daily routine with a bit more mindfulness. When I got into my car, I resolved to focus on driving thoughtfully instead of racing to make up for lost time. I made it a point to stop fully at each stop sign as a personal exercise in patience and presence. By slowing down and committing to each moment as it came, I felt calmer and more in control. Even my attitude toward traffic softened a bit. Instead of feeling constantly anxious to "get ahead," I started viewing my time on the road as a moment to regroup and center myself, rather than just a period to endure.

The irony was not lost on me. By slowing down and paying more attention, I actually felt more efficient, less flustered, and, oddly enough, less late overall. It was as if my speeding mistake had recalibrated something fundamental in me. I'd learned that my time—and my peace of mind—were too valuable to sacrifice for a few seconds saved on the road.

From that experience onward, I began to welcome my small mistakes as opportunities for growth rather than as inconveniences. Whether it's missing a turn, choosing the wrong lane, or even getting a ticket, each mistake holds a lesson if we're open to seeing it. With this mindset, my driving habits—and my approach to daily life—shifted in subtle yet profound ways. I became a little more patient, a little more forgiving of my own imperfections, and a little more aware of the fact that every mistake carries a seed of wisdom.

As I look back on that night, I'm grateful for that police stop, as strange as it may sound. It was the nudge I needed to step out of autopilot, to rethink how I approached each moment. The experience taught me that it's okay to make mistakes as long as we're willing to learn from them, to grow a bit wiser, and to apply that wisdom the next time around. That's the hope anyway." ;)   *–James WH*

The Rearview

Mistakes are often seen as setbacks, but in many spiritual, psychological, and philosophical traditions, they are considered essential catalysts for growth. As Marcus Aurelius put it, *"The impediment to action advances action. What stands in the way becomes the way."* Each mistake is not merely a hurdle but a stepping stone toward personal mastery.

Psychologically, the process of learning from mistakes aligns with Growth Mindset Theory, which emphasizes viewing challenges and errors as part of the journey to self-improvement. Carol Dweck's research highlights that embracing mistakes fosters adaptability, creativity, and long-term success. By reframing errors as lessons, we liberate ourselves from the fear of failure and open the door to continuous learning.

In Hinduism, the concept of karma reflects how mistakes and their consequences are integral to our spiritual journey. Far from being punishments, these outcomes are seen as lessons that guide us toward greater wisdom and self-awareness. The *Bhagavad Gita* teaches that all actions, even those resulting in errors, can lead to growth when approached with reflection and humility. Krishna advises, "No one becomes perfect by simply avoiding action" (Gita 3:4). Mistakes are inevitable, but they serve as a mirror, helping us recognize where our choices diverge from our values and encouraging us to realign with our dharma—our unique path of duty and righteousness.

In daily life, this means shifting our relationship with perfectionism and allowing ourselves to embrace imperfection. The experience of being pulled over for speeding could have been a purely negative memory, but by choosing to reflect and learn, it became a turning point. Whether on the road or in other aspects of life, rushing through moments often leads to missed opportunities for presence and growth. Each mistake holds a mirror to our tendencies, offering a chance to recalibrate and move forward with greater awareness.

Pixar Animation Studios, the American studio known for its critically and commercially successful feature films (*Toy Story, Monsters, Inc, Cars*) is known for their oft repeated in-house mantras "fail early and fail fast" and "be wrong as fast as you can."

In his book *Creativity, Inc.: Overcoming the Unseen Forces That Stand in the Way of True Inspiration*, CEO and co-founder Ed Catmull regularly returns to the notion of mistakes and Pixar's cultural response to failure. "We must remember that failure gives us chances to grow, and we ignore those chances at our own peril", he says. He also advises us to, "Turn pain into progress. To be wrong as fast as you can is to sign up for aggressive, rapid learning."

Ultimately, mistakes remind us of our humanity and capacity for transformation. As we slow down and pay closer attention to our choices, we not only avoid repeating the same errors but also cultivate a deeper wisdom. Life doesn't demand perfection; it asks only that we show up, learn, and grow—one moment at a time.

Suggested reading: *Oops!: The Art of Learning from Mistakes and Adventures* by Kent Sterling

CHAPTER EIGHT

Instant Karma

"When you truly understand karma, then you realize you are responsible for everything in your life."
— *Keanu Reeves*

In traffic, we often witness examples of instant karma: a driver who speeds past you only to be stopped at the next red light, or someone who cuts you off and immediately gets stuck in a slower lane. These moments can serve as powerful reminders of the immediate consequences of our actions and the interconnectedness of our experiences.

Instant karma teaches us that our actions have boomerang effects and that behaving with integrity and consideration often leads to more positive outcomes. It highlights the importance of mindfulness and the impact of our choices on ourselves and others. Recognizing these moments can inspire us to act with greater awareness and kindness, knowing that what we put out into the world often comes back to us.

Road Rage Goes Viral

In the busy streets of Melbourne, Australia, a dashcam captured a moment that would soon spread across the globe, becoming a cautionary tale of instant karma. The video opens with an all-too-familiar scene: bumper-to-bumper traffic crawling along, the frustration in the air almost palpable. Drivers impatiently inch forward, their eyes scanning the lanes for any opportunity to shave off even a few precious seconds. Among them, one vehicle suddenly swerves, cutting off another car. The driver of the offended vehicle honks, and that's when the situation escalates.

The enraged driver, who is clearly seething, pulls over, flings open his door, and storms out. His target is the car he cut off, and he's skipping–yes, he's aggressively skipping!– a beeline for the driver's side window, fists clenched, face contorted in a maniacal anger. The tension is electric. We've all seen this kind of scenario unfold: the moment when frustration bubbles over and transforms into wild road rage. Spectators might wonder what pushed him to this extreme. Was it a bad day at work? An argument at home? Or simply the endless tide of traffic?

He reaches the other car, now shouting, pointing, his anger a torrent of accusations. It's a scene of vulnerability for the driver inside—trapped in their vehicle, confronted by raw hostility. The situation feels on the brink of spiraling out of control.

But then, in a twist no screenwriter could script better, two figures appear from behind camera. Unbeknownst to him, a police car had been in the same traffic jam. Two officers step out, walking calmly yet purposefully. The camera captures their approach, unnoticed at first. There's an almost cinematic quality to the slow reveal—the officers emerging from the sidelines, the road rage driver oblivious until it's too late.

Finally, he senses their presence. The instant shift in his demeanor is almost comical. The bravado evaporates as quickly as it had flared up. He sees the officers, the realization hits and he turns to run back to his car. His aggression, his attempt to intimidate another driver, has backfired spectacularly. The officers don't hesitate; they move to detain him. His panicked attempt to flee is cut short and he's tackled and handcuffed, right there in the road, in full view of the gridlocked traffic he'd sought to dominate.

The entire scene—every second of it—was captured by the dashcam. When the video hit social media platforms, it spread like wildfire. On TikTok alone, it garnered millions of views within days. Comment sections buzzed with reactions ranging from schadenfreude to reflections on the nature of, you guessed it, instant karma. Many viewers shared their own tales of witnessing road rage and wondered aloud why some people let minor frustrations boil over into reckless confrontations.

The story resonates deeply because it taps into a universal truth: actions have consequences. In this case, the aggressive driver didn't have to wait long to face his. The officers' timely arrival transformed what could have been an intimidating and dangerous encounter into a powerful lesson—both for him and for everyone who watched the video.

What makes this incident particularly poignant is its symbolism. The highway, a place where we often feel isolated inside our metal boxes, where anonymity sometimes fuels impunity, became the setting for a dramatic reminder that accountability can be just around the corner. It also underscores how moments of anger and aggression are not just isolated flashes; they ripple out, impacting others, and can quickly rebound on the aggressor.

In the end, this viral video is more than just a moment of poetic justice. It's a call for self-awareness. It invites us to consider how we handle frustration and where those split-second decisions can lead. For the millions who watched, it was a reminder that in life—especially on the road—patience and calm are not just virtues but safeguards. Because you never know when your actions might come full circle, with an audience ready to learn from your mistakes.   – www

The Rearview

This incident offers a stark reminder of the inevitability of consequences. Across

spiritual traditions, the concept of *karma* aligns with fundamental teachings about the interconnectedness of actions and their outcomes.

From a Christian perspective, the principle of sowing and reaping is especially relevant. In Galatians 6:7, Paul writes, *"Do not be deceived: God cannot be mocked. A man reaps what he sows."* This verse reminds us that our actions—whether kind or not so much—inevitably bear fruit, often reflecting the choices we've made. The aggressive driver in this story reaped the consequences of his anger almost immediately, offering a modern example of this biblical truth. Christianity also emphasizes forgiveness and transformation, teaching that mistakes and poor choices can serve as opportunities for repentance, growth, and realignment with God's will.

Similarly, in Indigenous philosophies, the emphasis on harmony and balance reminds us that our actions ripple outward, impacting others and returning to us. Among the teachings of the Lakota Sioux, the idea of the *Sacred Hoop* or *Medicine Wheel* symbolizes life as a continuous cycle. When someone disrupts this harmony, the natural order seeks to restore balance, often with a lesson for those involved.

From a psychological perspective, the situation highlights the importance of emotional regulation. Aggression often stems from unprocessed stress or frustration. This incident shows how unchecked emotions can escalate a minor irritation into a life-altering event. Instead, practicing self-awareness and pausing to reflect in tense moments can prevent impulsive reactions and their unintended consequences.

The dashcam video serves as a cautionary tale and an opportunity for introspection. In a world where every action might be witnessed, recorded, and shared, it's a call to embody patience, mindfulness, and accountability—to contribute to a more compassionate and harmonious environment. At the very least to avoid global public humiliation!

In the immortal words of American singer Brit Smith, "Karma's a bitch, and she's with you right now."

Suggested reading: *Karma Manual: 9 Days to Change Your Life* by Jonn Mumford

CHAPTER NINE

Be Like Water

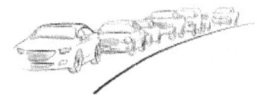

"Adaptability is about the powerful difference between adapting to cope and adapting to win."
– Max McKeown

Navigating the roads of Los Angeles requires both flexibility and adaptability as well as a willingness to occasionally bail on your plans completely. We learn that the quickest way to our destination is not always the most direct. Sometimes taking side streets or alternative routes can save time and offer a more pleasant journey. Traffic jams, road closures, and construction can force us to adapt and explore new paths, teaching us the importance of being flexible and open to change.

In life, as on the road, there are many ways to achieve our goals. Being open to detours and unexpected routes can lead to surprising discoveries and opportunities. Flexibility allows us to navigate challenges with more ease and find new paths when the old ones are blocked. As we've seen, choosing the scenic route can teach us to appreciate the journey itself, not just the destination. It encourages us to be present and open to new experiences, finding beauty and value in the unexpected.

Embracing this mindset can lead to greater fulfillment and a deeper understanding of the world around us. By being flexible and willing to explore new routes, we can find joy and growth in the journey, no matter how winding it may be.

Embracing The Path Of Least Resistance

"One Friday evening, I found myself in a familiar situation: bumper-to-bumper traffic on the way home from work. My go-to route—the straight shot down the 101 to Silverlake Boulevard—was absolutely packed. This was the pre-GPS days when "Thomas" was our Guide, and I was reluctant to deviate from my usual path. After all, it was a strong habit; I knew every exit, every sign, every lane change by now. But that night, as I sat idle watching brake lights stretch on in a seemingly endless line, I decided to try something new. I felt a twinge of excitement and a little trepidation; embarking on this unknown journey. So, I took a spontaneous right off the exit and onto a winding route through the hills.

At first, I was hyper-aware of each turn, trying to memorize the landmarks as I passed. This wasn't the quickest way to my destination, at least by mileage, but after just a few blocks, I was already noticing something refreshing: I was actually moving. There were no long stretches of stationary brake lights, no honking, no revving of engines. I could actually feel my grip on the wheel loosen, and I let out a sigh of relief. As I maneuvered through the narrow streets and rolling hills, I caught glimpses of the city from new angles. I passed by quaint, tucked-away neighborhoods and saw views of the skyline

I'd never noticed before. My commute began to feel less like a race and more like a deliberate, almost meditative, drive through the city, with KROQ providing the evening's soundtrack.

The further I went, the more my outlook shifted. I began noticing architectural gems tucked away among the trees, small cafes with open patios, and even a street musician busking outside a tiny park. One of the things that I love most about Los Angeles is its diverse and creative architecture and, in that moment, it struck me how much I had been missing by sticking to the same route day in and day out. The more rigid my routine, the narrower my view had become. By embracing a less direct path, I had unlocked a part of the city—and perhaps a part of myself—that I'd been overlooking.

With each turn, I felt more connected to the world around me. I was discovering details, people, and sights that I'd previously missed by rushing past. The scenic route offered a chance to appreciate the nuances of life in a way that the express lanes simply didn't allow. A winding road might take a bit longer, but it also provided something invaluable: perspective. It reminded me that sometimes, slowing down and taking in our surroundings can lead us to unexpected joy.

As I reached my Silverlake apartment that evening, I realized that I hadn't just stumbled upon a new way home—I'd discovered a fresh approach to life.

The quickest route isn't always the most fulfilling one. Life, like driving, doesn't need to be a relentless pursuit of the "straightest path" between two points. There is value in the detours, the side streets, and the moments when we choose to see what lies just beyond our usual comfort zone.

Since that night, I've made it a habit to explore alternative routes whenever possible, both on the road and in life. Instead of being beholden to the destination, I've learned to embrace the journey, with all its curves and turns. Every time I find a new hidden gem—be it a park, a mural, or a roadside cafe—I'm reminded of the rewards that come from letting go of the urge to rush. Flexibility, it turns out, isn't just a way to navigate the road; it's a way to navigate life itself." – James WH

The Rearview

The choice to veer off the beaten path that evening wasn't just a change in scenery—it was a shift in perspective. That spontaneous decision to explore a winding route through the hills reflected a profound truth about flexibility and adaptation: often, the detours enrich our journey in ways the main road never could.

For the Taoist, this experience aligns beautifully with the, now familiar, concept of *wu wei*, or effortless action. Taoism encourages us to flow with the natural currents of life, much like water moving around obstacles rather than fighting against them. By choosing an alternate route, we step into this practice—embracing a path of least resistance and finding harmony in the present moment.

In Judaism, the idea of flexibility and embracing life's unexpected paths resonates with the principle of *bitachon* ("trust"), specifically trust in G*D or *Hashem* ("The Name"). Bitachon teaches us to have faith that the detours and challenges we face are part of a larger, divine plan. By taking an unfamiliar route, we symbolically step into the space of trust, letting go of the need to control every aspect of my journey. This mindset reflects the wisdom found in *Pirkei Avot* (Ethics of the Fathers), an ancient collection of Jewish ethical teachings. The first *Mishna*, or lesson, ends with the warning to "be patient in judgment" and see situations through a broader, spiritual lens. When we instead embrace the unknown with trust and curiosity, we often uncover beauty and meaning we would have otherwise missed.

And, finally, from a scientific standpoint, the experience ties into the study of neuroplasticity—the brain's remarkable ability to adapt and reorganize itself in response to new experiences. When we break out of our habitual commutes, we activate neural pathways associated with curiosity, problem-solving, and creativity. Research shows that such deviations from routine can enhance cognitive flexibility and even increase resilience. Taking that different route wasn't just a change of scenery; it was an exercise in expanding mental adaptability, opening the mind to fresh possibilities and reducing stress through novelty.

Together, these perspectives remind us that stepping away from well-worn, tired patterns can lead to profound transformation. The detours we take, both literal and metaphorical, invite us to deepen our understanding of ourselves and the world, fostering a life that is both richer and more resilient.

Suggested reading: *Elastic: Flexible Thinking in a Time of Change* by Leonard Mlodinow

CHAPTER TEN

Trail Angels

"Unexpected kindness is the most powerful, least costly, and most underrated agent of human change."
– Bob Kerre

In the hustle and bustle of Los Angeles traffic, moments of unexpected kindness can be like encountering angels on the road. Whether it's a stranger letting you merge into a lane during rush hour or someone offering help when your car breaks down, these acts of generosity remind us of the goodness in humanity and the power of compassion.

Encountering angels on the road teaches us to be grateful for the kindness shown to us and inspires us to look for opportunities to pay it forward. Whether it's offering a smile to a stressed-out driver, letting someone merge in front of us, or simply being patient and courteous in traffic, each of us has the power to be that angel for someone else. By consciously choosing to spread positivity and compassion on the road, we not only create a more harmonious driving experience but also contribute to a ripple effect of kindness that extends beyond our immediate surroundings. Let us strive to be the unexpected source of light and kindness in someone else's day, knowing that our actions can make a meaningful difference in the world around us.

The Angel On The Highway

"Freeway traffic in Los Angeles can feel like a test of patience, endurance, and sometimes, faith in humanity. On this particular day, the freeway was a nightmare—stop-and-go congestion that stretched for miles, the kind of jam where every inch gained feels like a small victory. Horns blared, tempers flared, and you could almost feel the collective frustration hanging in the air.

I was already running late, my mood souring with every red brake light ahead. As I approached the on-ramp, I noticed a pickup truck trying to merge into the endless line of cars. The driver glanced over with a stoic expression, probably expecting the usual L.A. treatment: a cold shoulder and zero eye contact. But something in me decided in that moment to go another way today. Maybe it was the look of quiet determination on his face, or perhaps I was just tired of the constant competition on these roads. Whatever it was, I eased back, flashed my lights and let him slip into the lane ahead of me.

He nodded in acknowledgment as he joined the slow-moving river of traffic and eventually I lost sight of him among the sea of vehicles. I didn't think much of it; after all, it was just a small gesture. No big deal.

Eventually, I couldn't take the gridlock anymore. My gas gauge was dipping low, and I needed a break. I pulled off at the next exit, aiming for a nearby gas station. I parked, got out, and started fueling up. As the pump clicked into place, I heard the low rumble of an engine pulling in behind me. I glanced up, and there he was—the guy from the freeway. His truck rolled to a stop, and he climbed out.

I'll admit, for a split second, my mind raced. He was a big dude, built like a linebacker, and I had no idea why he'd followed me. My heart rate ticked up as he walked toward me, his face serious. But then, he extended his hand.

"Thanks, man," he said, his voice deep but warm. "I just wanted to say thanks for letting me in back there. Everyone else drives like a selfish dick around here, but you didn't. Thank you."

I shook his hand, still a little surprised. "Did you really stop just to tell me that?" I asked, allowing a smile to creep onto my face.

"Yeah," he said, nodding. "I had to. It meant something."

We stood there for a moment, the noise of the freeway humming in the background. I couldn't help but think he must not be from around here. Most L.A. drivers wouldn't go out of their way to say thank you. As he turned back toward his truck, I caught a glimpse of his license plate: Michigan. Of course. My own homestate.

As he drove off, I stood there, reflecting on the moment. In the chaos of the freeway, amidst the frustration and the selfishness, this guy had taken the time to acknowledge a simple act of kindness. He didn't have to. He could've merged and forgotten about it, like most of us would. But he didn't.

It struck me that these little gestures—letting someone merge, offering a smile, saying thank you—are like ripples in the water. They seem small, almost insignificant, but they can change the entire current. In that brief interaction, we both felt a bit of grace, a moment of human connection in the most unlikely of places.

Driving in L.A. can make you cynical. Hard. Even a road-raging asshole. It's easy to assume the worst about people, to see only the selfishness and aggression. But sometimes, an angel appears on the highway—not with wings or a halo, but with a simple thank you. And sometimes, that angel can be you.

As I got back into my car, I felt a little lighter. The traffic hadn't disappeared, and I was still running late. But the frustration had melted away. That big guy from Michigan- I didn't even get his name- reminded me that kindness isn't just something we give; it's something we pass along. And on a congested freeway, a little kindness can go a long way.

Also, Michiganders really are the best people in the country!" – Michael K.

The Rearview

In Judaism, the concept of *chesed*—loving-kindness—underscores the idea that even the smallest acts of compassion can ripple outward, creating transformative effects in the world. Chesed is not just an individual virtue but a communal responsibility, an acknowledgment that we are all interconnected. In the moment Michael let the pickup truck merge, he practiced chesed, a simple yet profound act of kindness that created an unexpected connection.

The *Talmud* teaches, "Whoever saves a single life is as though they have saved the entire world" (Sanhedrin 37a). While this wisdom applies most directly to acts of life-saving, it also reminds us of the profound impact of every action, no matter how small. A kind gesture, like letting a driver into a lane or expressing gratitude, holds the power to uplift both the giver and the recipient. Such acts reflect the divine spark within each of us, bridging the divides that often make us feel separate.

Just as the driver from Michigan made the effort to acknowledge Michael's small kindness, he perpetuated a cycle of grace that transformed a mundane moment into a memorable one. This ripple effect of chesed serves as a reminder: we all have the ability to act as "angels" in each other's lives, guiding each other through life's congestion with simple, meaningful gestures.

Physiologically, acts of kindness trigger a variety of positive reactions in the brain and body, creating a cascading loop effect that can influence both the giver and the recipient. Research in the fields of neuroscience and psychology shows that performing kind acts can stimulate the release of neurochemicals such as oxytocin, serotonin, and endorphins, all of which are associated with feelings of happiness, connection, and reduced stress.

For example, studies have shown that when we perform acts of kindness, our brain's reward center, particularly the ventral striatum, becomes active, which is linked to feelings of pleasure and satisfaction. This neurological reward reinforces prosocial behavior, motivating us to continue engaging in acts that benefit others (Aknin et al., 2013). Furthermore, when we engage in compassionate actions, oxytocin, often referred to as the "love hormone," is released. This hormone not only helps to reduce stress but also promotes social bonding and trust, which can lead to a sense of interconnectedness and community.

The recipient of a kind act also experiences physiological benefits. In a study conducted by researchers at the University of California, Berkeley, it was found that those who received help from others showed a decrease in their blood pressure and cortisol levels, as well as an increase in heart rate variability, which is an indicator of better heart health (Brown et al., 2003). These findings suggest that kindness may reduce stress, contribute to overall well-being and even increase longevity for both the giver and the receiver.

Thus, from a scientific viewpoint, kindness creates a biological feedback loop that not only benefits the individuals directly involved but also enhances the general social environment by promoting positive, nurturing interactions. These acts, however small, can lead to a broader sense of community, wellbeing, and even improved health.

By understanding this physiological feedback loop, we see that kindness isn't just a moral choice but also, dare I say, a biological imperative!

Suggested reading: *The Kindness Diaries: One Man's Quest to Ignite Goodwill and Transform Lives Around the World* by Leon Logothetis

BONUS CHAPTER

Practicing Gratitude

"Gratitude is not only the greatest of virtues but the parent of all others."
– Cicero

In the midst of traffic, it's easy to focus on the negatives – the delays, the congestion, the stress. But there is always something to be grateful for. Perhaps you have a comfortable car, a job to go to, or loved ones to return to. By shifting your focus to gratitude, you can transform your experience of traffic from one of frustration to one of appreciation.

Practicing gratitude in traffic is a powerful spiritual exercise that can enhance your overall sense of well-being. It reminds us to focus on the positive aspects of our lives, even in challenging situations. Gratitude can shift our mindset from one of lack to one of abundance, helping us to see and appreciate the many blessings we have.

Gratitude In Gridlock

"It was one of those long drives back from the coast on a gridlocked I-10 in Los Angeles, where the sea of red brake lights stretched endlessly ahead. I was on my way home to Pasadena after a long day working a commercial on Venice Beach. As I sighed and checked the clock, again, I could feel frustration creeping in, the usual nagging voice wondering how much longer I'd be stuck here. I wanted to get home.

I wanted a shower, food and sleep. Not necessarily in that order. And yet, here I was, bumper to bumper with hundreds of others, all in the same boat.

But then, out of nowhere, a thought hit me: what if I stopped fighting this moment? What if, instead of treating this drive like an obstacle, I treated it as an opportunity?

See! I was learning, right?

After all, I had the luxury of a safe, comfortable car. I had music at my fingertips, a clear view of the setting sun to my right, and the freedom to go where I pleased. Somehow, in the chaos of my daily routines, I had forgotten to appreciate all of that. This standstill could be a reminder, a nudge to see my journey differently. I decided to try something: instead of grumbling through this drive, I would look for things to be thankful for.

I took a deep breath, letting it out slowly, and looked around. I noticed a couple laughing together in the next lane over, both their heads thrown back as if sharing some inside joke. Despite the traffic, they looked utterly at peace. Their laughter filled their car, as if they had all the time in the world. I caught myself smiling, reminded that joy wasn't exclusive to perfect moments. The mundane could be beautiful, too. And hadn't my years as an Army Ranger taught me that humor could even be found in the hardest of times.

Shifting my focus, I turned to the view outside my window to the left. I had a clear look at the downtown skyline bathed in the warm, golden light of late afternoon. In any other circumstance, I would have ignored it, my eyes glued to the road ahead. But here, forced to slow down, I could really take it in, savoring how lucky I was to live in a city that so many people dream of visiting. The noise, the people, the rush—all of it was part of the unique character of this place. How many times had I longed for moments of beauty like this, only to miss them because I was too busy racing from one thing to the next?

As my car inched forward, I found myself feeling more at ease. I was in no rush; I would get there when I got there. I thought of my car itself, the first car I had ever purchased brand new off the lot and was still only a couple years old. I remembered relying on public transportation not long ago, waiting in the cold for buses, and hoping for a seat. This car was a dream come true at one point. And I was still that same person, grateful just to have it.

Then I thought of all the people who didn't have the luxury to drive, who couldn't hop in a car to get home or see loved ones whenever they pleased. Traffic was an annoyance, sure, but it was also a sign of my freedom and independence. Each person around me had their own journey, their own reasons for being on this stretch of road. We were all in it together, a moving—and sometimes unmoving—

community of travelers, with our own destinations and stories.

By the time I finally started moving at a decent pace, something had shifted. I didn't feel the usual pressure to get there as quickly as possible. My drive had been transformed, not because traffic had let up, but because I had chosen to see it differently. I realized that gratitude wasn't about waiting for perfect moments. It was about finding peace and appreciation, even when things didn't go as planned. This simple change in perspective made my commute easier, sure, but it also made me feel calmer, more present, and oddly fulfilled.

Since then I've made gratitude my go-to strategy, not just for traffic but for life. I remind myself that no matter the circumstances, there's always something to be thankful for. The car, the road, the city, and even the congestion—each is a piece of the journey, teaching me to slow down, look around, and appreciate the ride. *–James WH*

The Rearview

In the midst of life's daily challenges, especially the ones that seem to stretch our patience—like being stuck in traffic—practicing gratitude can be a transformative tool. It can also be a bit of a challenge to muster. It can help to think of gratitude as a muscle that becomes easier to flex the more that it's exercised.

Psychologically, gratitude is linked to improved mental health, as it shifts our focus from what we lack to what we already have, fostering positive emotions and reducing stress (Emmons & McCullough, 2003). This simple yet powerful shift in perspective doesn't just enhance our emotional well-being, it can change how we engage with the world around us. Research by Robert A. Emmons and Michael E. McCullough has shown that people who practice gratitude report higher levels of happiness and lower levels of depression, especially when gratitude is practiced regularly.

Most spiritual practices recognize the transformative power of gratitude, though the emphasis and expression may vary across traditions. Gratitude is widely seen as a way to foster spiritual growth, humility, and connection with the divine or with others.

In Buddhism gratitude is often linked with mindfulness and the practice of metta (loving-kindness). By recognizing the interconnectedness of all beings, practitioners are encouraged to feel thankful for the support, love, and even the challenges they receive in life. This fosters compassion and reduces attachment to negative emotions.

Gratitude is core tenet of Christianity, often seen as a direct response to God's gifts. The *Bible* encourages believers to give thanks in all circumstances and to view gratitude as an expression of faith and humility. Gratitude in this context often connects with the practice of prayer and worship.

In Islam, gratitude or *shukr* is one of the core virtues. Muslims are taught to be thankful for the blessings of Allah, both in times of prosperity and hardship. The Qur'an emphasizes gratitude as a key to further divine blessings, encouraging believers to show gratitude through actions, such as helping others and being mindful of the needs of the less fortunate (Qur'an, 14:7).

According to Hindu philosophy, gratitude is essential in acknowledging the divine presence in every aspect of life. The practice of giving thanks is often tied to devotion (*bhakti*) and rituals where offerings of gratitude are made to gods, ancestors, and the universe. The Bhagavad Gita also emphasizes the importance of selfless service and being grateful for life's lessons.

And, of course, many Indigenous spiritual traditions recognize the importance of gratitude as part of a reciprocal relationship with the Earth and all living beings. Gratitude is expressed through offerings, prayers, and acts of stewardship, where the natural world is viewed as a sacred and interconnected whole. The Native American tradition, for example, often emphasizes the practice of giving thanks to the land, animals, and ancestors as an act of honoring their contributions.

Gratitude, in these varied spiritual traditions, is not just about acknowledgment but is often intertwined with acts of service, mindfulness, and devotion, turning gratitude into both a practice and a way of moving through the world. Whether in the context of connecting to a higher power, fostering compassion for others, or simply embracing life's blessings, gratitude is a universally recognized and powerful force across spiritual and philosophical systems.

Gratitude isn't about waiting for perfect conditions but about finding appreciation in the imperfect moments. This shift not only improves how we feel about individual situation, it can also reframe our entire approach to life, turning every moment into an opportunity for gratitude, growth, and gnosis.

Suggested reading: *Thanks!: How the New Science of Gratitude Can Make You Happier by* Robert A. Emmons AND *Gratitude: A Way of Life* by Louise Hay

Conclusion

"Things just happen in the right way, at the right time. At least when you let them, when you work with circumstances instead of saying, 'This isn't supposed to be happening this way,' and trying harder to make it happen some other way." – Benjamin Hoff, The Tao of Pooh

As we reach the end of our journey together we can reflect on the profound teachings hidden within the seemingly mundane experiences of our daily commutes. From patience in gridlock to the power of unexpected kindness, each lesson offers a unique perspective on how we can grow spiritually amidst the chaos of traffic. These moments on the road are not just about getting from here to there; they are opportunities to practice mindfulness, compassion, flexibility, and gratitude.

Through the hustle and bustle of Los Angeles traffic, we've learned to embrace the journey rather than just the destination. We've discovered the importance of letting go of control, adapting to change, and seeing the bigger picture. We've found that the quickest route is not always the most direct and that there are many ways to reach our goals if we remain open and flexible. We've also recognized the significance and power of breath in finding inner peace.

Most importantly, we've come to understand, just as Robert Frost once did, that the road is a metaphor for life itself. The challenges and obstacles we face on our commutes mirror those we encounter in our daily lives. By applying these spiritual lessons to our time on the road, we can cultivate a more mindful, compassionate, and fulfilling existence. Every traffic jam, red light, and rude gesture becomes an opportunity for growth and self-discovery.

As you continue your journey, remember to look for the lesson in every experience, whether you're behind the wheel or navigating the complexities of life. Be patient, stay present, and embrace the unexpected. Let go of judgment, trust the process, and be kind to others. By doing so, you'll not only transform your driving experience but also enrich your life in countless ways.

Safe travels, and may you find peace and enlightenment on the roads ahead.

Suggested reading: *The Tao of Pooh* by Benjamin Hoff

Acknowledgements

As I said at the start, I never expected to write this book. I mean, I get LOTS of book ideas but had never followed through with any of them until now. Perhaps this is the start of another author's career? Who knows. But I do know who to thank for providing the impetus to get this one out into the world.

It was over dinner with friends Dan Radlauer and Karen Biers at their lovely vintage Hollywood home in Brentwood, CA. I mentioned, off-hand, that I had this book idea bouncing around my brain for a few years and had even made some notes–chapter headings really–that were written down somewhere.

After I spent a minute or two describing it with a couple examples, they both, nearly in unison, exclaimed that "You have to write that book!"

Apparently that's all I needed to hear as I started work on it within the week.

Thank you for the nudge guys. I hope you like the results.

I also need to acknowledge that no creative work

is born in a vacuum; at least not for me. That is especially true in this case. Being my first book, there was quite a learning curve as I navigated my way through all the ins and outs of self publication including editing, proofreading, cover design, formatting, obtaining an ISBN, copyright registration, marketing strategy, and distribution to name but a few.

I had a lot of teachers to walk me through the various steps. Thank you YouTube Creators. You really can learn anything on that platform.

Lastly, a huge Thank You to my beta readers, Zane Levitt, Michael Kallio, Lisa Biggar, and Evan Nichols. You have all made this much better (and longer!) than the book I initially set out to make.

Thank You!

I hope you found *Road Rage to Road Sage* valuable and inspiring. If you enjoyed it, **_please consider leaving a review_** on Amazon or wherever else you may have found the book. Your feedback helps others discover the title and supports my work in exponential ways. Thank you for your time and thoughts. They- YOU- mean the world!

Tune-Up Topics

Just as cars need regular maintenance, these questions and prompts are designed to help you tune up your mindful awareness and balance your emotional engine, facilitating a smoother, more intentional drive through life.

1. Think about your last frustrating commute or long wait. What could you have done in that moment to shift your mindset? Or, what DID you do?
   - Identify one new habit you could adopt for the next time this happens.

2. Consider a moment when you experienced an unexpected act of kindness. How did it make you feel? How can you pay that feeling forward in your daily life?

3. The book encourages flexibility in the face of detours. What is one "detour" in your life right now, and how can you embrace it as part of your journey?

4. Reflect on the last time you felt overwhelmed by external circumstances (e.g.

traffic, deadlines or disagreements). How can you use breath or mindfullness techniques to find calm in similar situations?
- Identify one new habit you could adopt for the next time this happens.
- Practice a simple breath exercise and note how it changes your mood.

5. What are three small things you can do tomorrow to make your commute or daily routine more meaningful? These could include listening to an inspiring podcast, reaching out to someone with kindness, or practicing gratitude.

6. Was there a time when you acted as an "angel on the road" for someone else? How did that experience shape your day?
- Commit to one small act of kindness in the coming week and observe its impact.

7. Think of an area of your life where you are resisting change or release of control. What would letting go look like, and what is one small step you could take toward surrendering to the flow?

8. The book emphasizes gratitude as a way to reframe challenges. Write down five things you are grateful for, even if they seem small or mundane. How does this practice shift your

perspective?
- Consider this as a daily exercise for a while.

9. When was the last time you truly noticed your surroundings during an ordinary activity? What can you do to be more present and mindful in everyday moments?
- Take five minutes today to observe the world around you and jot down what you notice.

10. If traffic symbolizes life's shared struggles, what is one way you can foster connection with others in your community or workplace?
- Plan a specific action, like sharing a meal, offering help, or striking up a conversation with someone you don't usually talk to.

Appendix A

Box Breathing (Square Breathing) – This technique helps to focus your mind and regulate stress.

1. Inhale deeply through your nose for 4 counts.
2. Hold your breath for 4 counts.
3. Exhale slowly through your mouth for 4 counts.
4. Hold your breath again for 4 counts.
5. Repeat the cycle 3-5 times or until you feel more grounded.

The 5-5-7 Breath – This method emphasizes extending the exhale, which promotes relaxation.

1. Inhale deeply through your nose for 5 counts.
2. Hold your breath gently for 5 counts.
3. Exhale slowly through your mouth for 7 counts, focusing on the feeling of release.
4. Repeat for 1-2 minutes, or as long as it feels comfortable.

Alternate Nostril Breathing (Nadi Shodhana) – A calming and balancing breath often used in yoga.

1. Sit comfortably and use your right thumb to gently close your right nostril.
2. Inhale slowly through your left nostril.
3. Close your left nostril with your ring finger and release your thumb from the right nostril.
4. Exhale slowly through the right nostril.

5. Inhale through the right nostril, then switch sides, exhaling through the left nostril.
6. Continue alternating nostrils for 1-3 minutes.

About The Author

James Wilderhancock

James WilderHancock fell into the film business in the early 90's after several weeks of cold calling and mailing resumes to production companies near and far. His first film opportunity found him in Southern Oregon as an unpaid intern on a Grizzly Adams picture. By the end of that three-week gig, he was the Best Boy Grip and shortly received an invitation to Tinsel Town to work on a real Hollywood production.

James recently pivoted from his technical expertise behind the camera to focus more on the creative side as a writer and producer. This transition marks a new chapter, driven by a lifelong passion for storytelling.

He has served on the board of the Oregon Media Production Association, is a founding member of the Oregon Producers Alliance, and is also a plankholder of the 3rd Battalion, 75th Ranger Regiment, stationed in Ft. Moore, GA. He is currently developing a project based on those years spent building a special operations unit from the ground up.

linkedin.com/in/wilderhancock/
FB @James WilderHancock
instagram.com/wilderhancock/

www.ingramcontent.com/pod-product-compliance
Lightning Source LLC
Chambersburg PA
CBHW071301040426
42444CB00009B/1814